MASSINAHIGAN SERIES

Brief Accounts of Early Native America

Vol. 2

"You have your Massinahigan; *(that is to say,
you have a knowledge of writing),
which makes you remember everything."*

—An Algonquin captain to Champlain at Quebec,
1633. The *Jesuit Relations*, Vol. 5, p. 207.

SKETCHES OF
ANCIENT HISTORY
OF THE
SIX NATIONS

by

David Cusick

Evolution Publishing
Merchantville, New Jersey

This edition extracted from:

William M. Beauchamp. 1892. *The Iroquois trail, or Foot-prints of the Six Nations in customs, traditions, and history...in which are included David Cusick's Sketches of ancient history of the Six Nations*. Printed by H.C. Beauchamp, Fayetteville, NY.

This edition ©2004, ©2024 Evolution Publishing
Merchantville, New Jersey.

Manufactured in the United States of America

Hardcover: ISBN 978-1-889758-58-9 (2004)
Paperback: ISBN: 978-1-935228-31-8 (2024)

Preface to the 2004 edition

Tuscarora historian David Cusick was aware of the two main shortcomings of his *Sketches of Ancient History of the Six Nations*, first published in 1825. The first was his being, as he charmingly put it "so small educated," with an irregular command of English and a peculiar literary style. The second was that the history of his people was "involved with fables." Among accounts of migrations and wars, are interspersed giants, flying heads, and a poisonous blue otter. Modern commentators have also pointed to the "fabulous" and "extravagant" chronology that undergirds this history, which attempts to relate events back to 1000 B.C.

These criticisms aside though, the true value in Cusick's book is in assembling chronologically the origin and historical traditions of the Iroquois people themselves. As pure fairy tales these would certainly be valuable enough—who would bear to part with Donhtonha and the giant? But it would be too rash to classify the whole as devoid of historical truth. Cusick's dates for the southern migration of the Tuscarora (A.D. 1), and the Iroquois proper becoming independent nations (A.D. 500) actually compare quite favorably with dates suggested by modern archaeologists and linguists, who place the Tuscarora split at 500 B.C.–A.D. 100, and the divergence of the Five Nations at A.D. 500–800.* On the other hand, his latter date is muddled with the founding of the Iroquois League, an event which probably took place 1000 years later. So while it would be unwise to demand precision from these traditions, they may well contain ancestral memories of actual prehistoric events, even if somewhat confused. With this possibility in mind, Cusick's dates in years before Columbus have been rounded and converted to dates of the Christian era and added in the margins.

With the understanding that these *Sketches* are part history, part legend, and part fable, this singular study in American antiquities is once again offered the public. If Cusick's chronology be extravagant, his prose stilted, nevertheless we owe him a great debt for so diligently collecting the oral traditions of his people and framing them into a single chronological narrative.

—Claudio R. Salvucci, ed.

* see the *Handbook of North American Indians*, Vol. 15 pp. 60-61; Vol. 17 pp. 105-106.

PREFACE.

I have been long waiting in hopes that some of my people, who have received an English education, would have undertaken the work as to give a sketch of the Ancient History of the Six Nations; but found no one seemed to concur in the matter, after some hesitation I determined to commence the work; but found the history involved with fables; and besides, examining myself, finding so small educated that it was impossible for me to compose the work without much difficulty. After various reasons I abandoned the idea; I however, took a resolution to continue the work, which I have taken much pains procuring the materials, and translating it into English language. I have endeavored to throw some light on the history of the original population of the country, which I believe never have been recorded. I hope this little work will be acceptable to the public.

Tuscarora Village, June 10th, 1825.

DAVID CUSICK.

PART I.

A Tale of the Foundation of the Great Island, now North America:—The two Infants born, and the Creation of the Universe.

Among the ancients there were two worlds in existence. The lower world was in a great darkness; the possession of the great monster; but the upper world was inhabited by mankind; and there was a woman conceived and would have the twin born. When her travail drew near, and her situation seemed to produce a great distress on her mind, and she was induced by some of her relatives to lay herself on a mattress which was prepared, so as to gain refreshments to her wearied body; but while she was asleep the very place sunk down towards the dark world. The monsters of the great water were alarmed at her appearance of descending to the lower world; in consequence, all the species of the creatures were immediately collected into where it was expected she would fall. When the monsters were assembled, and they made consultation, one of them was appointed in haste to search the great deep, in order to procure some earth, if it could be obtained; accordingly the monster descends, which succeeds, and returns to the place.

Another requisition was presented, who would be capable to secure the woman from the terrors of the great water, but none was able to comply except a large turtle came forward and made proposal to them to endure her lasting weight, which was accepted. The woman was yet descending from a great distance. The turtle executes upon the spot, and a small quantity of earth was varnished on the back of the turtle. The woman alights on the seat prepared, and receives a satisfaction. While holding her, the turtle increased every moment, and become a considerable island of earth, and apparently covered with small bushes. The woman remained in a state of unlimited darkness, and she was overtaken by her travail to which she was subject. While she was in the limits of distress one of the infants was moved by an evil opinion, and he was determined to pass out under the side of the parent's arm, and the other infant in vain endeavored to prevent his design. The woman was in a painful condition during the time of their disputes, and the infants entered the dark world by compulsion, and their parent expired in a few moments. They had the power of sustenance without a nurse and remained in the dark regions. After a time the turtle increased to a great Island, and the infants were grown up, and one of them possessed with a gentle disposition and named Enigorio, i.e. the good mind. The other youth possessed an insolence of character, and was named Enigonhahetgea, i.e. the bad mind. The good mind was not contented to remain in a dark situation, and he was anxious to create a great light in the dark world; but the bad mind was desirous, that the world should remain in a natural state. The good mind determined to prosecute his designs, and therefore commences the work of creation. At first he took the parent's head, (the deceased) of which he created an orb, and established it in the center of the firmament and it became of a very superior nature to bestow light to the new world, (now the sun) and again he took the remnant of the body, and formed another orb, which was inferior to the light, (now the moon.) In the orb a cloud of legs appeared to prove it was the body of the good mind, (parent.) The former was to give light to the day, and the latter to the night; and he also created numerous spots of light, (now stars;) these were to regulate the days, nights, seasons, years, etc. Whenever the light extended to the dark world the monsters were displeased and immediately concealed themselves in the deep places, lest they should be discovered by some human beings. The good mind continued the work, of creation, and he formed numerous creeks and rivers on the Great Island, and then created numerous species of animals of the smallest and greatest, to inhabit the forests, and fish of all kinds to inhabit the waters. When he had made the universe he was in doubt respecting some being to possess the Great Island; and he formed two images of the dust of the ground in his own likeness, male and female, and by his breathing into their nostrils he gave them the living souls, and named them Ea-gwe-howe, i.e. a real people; and he gave the Great Island, all the animals of game for their maintenance: and he appointed thunder to water the earth by frequent rains, agreeable to the nature of the system; after this the Island became fruitful, and vegetation afforded the animals subsistence. The bad mind, while his brother was making the Universe, went throughout the Island and made numerous high mountains and falls of water, and great steeps, and also creates various reptiles which would be injurious to mankind; but the good mind restored the Island to its former condition. The bad mind proceeded further in his motives, and he made two images of clay in the form of mankind; but while he was giving them existence they became apes; and when he had not the power to create mankind he was envious against his brother; and again he made two of clay. The good mind discovered his brother's contrivances, and aided in giving them living souls,* (It is said these had the most knowledge of good and evil.) The good mind now accomplishes the works of creation, notwithstanding the imaginations of the bad mind were continually evil; and he attempted to enclose all the animals of game in the earth, so as to deprive them from mankind; but the good mind released them from confinement, (the animals were dispersed, and traces of them were made on the rocks near the cave where it was closed.) The good mind experiences that his brother was at variance with the works of creation, and feels not disposed to favor any of his proceedings, but gives admonitions of his future state. Afterwards the good mind requested his brother to accompany him, as he was proposed to inspect the game, etc., but when a short distance from their nominal residence, the bad mind became so unmanly that he could not conduct his brother any more. The bad mind offered a challenge to his brother and resolved that who gains the victory should govern the universe; and appointed a day to meet the contest. The good mind was willing to submit to the offer, and he

---

* It appears by the fictitious accounts that the said beings become civilized people, and made their residence in the southern parts of the Island; but afterwards, they were destroyed by the barbarous nations, and their fortifications were ruined unto this day.

enters the reconciliation with his brother; which he falsely mentions that by whipping with flags would destroy his temporal life; and he earnestly solicits his brother also to notice the instrument of death, which he manifestly relates by the use of deer horns, beating his body he would expire. On the day appointed the engagement commenced, which lasted for two days; after pulling up the trees and mountains as the track of a terrible whirlwind, at last the good mind gains the victory by using the horns, as mentioned the instrument of death, which he succeeded in deceiving his brother, and he crushed him in the earth: and the last words uttered from the bad mind were, that he would have equal power over the souls of mankind after death: and he sinks down to eternal doom, and became the Evil Spirit. After this tumult the good mind repaired to the battle ground and then visited the people and retires from the earth.

PART II.

A real account of the settlement of
North America and their dissensions.

In the ancient days the Great Island appeared upon the big waters, the earth brought forth trees, herbs, vegetables, etc. the creation of the land animals; the Eagwehoewe people were too created, and resided in the north regions, and after a time some of the people become giants and committed outrages upon the inhabitants, etc. After many years a body of Eagwehoewe people encamped on the bank of a majestic stream, and was named *Kanawage*, now St. Lawrence. After a long time a number of foreign people sailed from a port unknown; but unfortunately before reached their destination the winds drove them contrary; at length their ship wrecked somewhere on the southern part of the Great Island, and many of the crews perished: a few active persons were saved: they obtained some implements and each of them was covered with a leather bag, the big hawks carried them on the summit of a mountain and remained there but a short time the hawks seemed to threaten them, and were compelled to leave the mountain. They immediately selected a place for residence and built a small fortification in order to provide against the attacks of furious beasts; if there should be any made. After many years the foreign people became numerous, and extended their settlements; but afterwards they were destroyed by the monsters that overrun the country. About this time the Eagwehoewe people inhabited on the river Kanawaga or St. Lawrence; but they could not enjoy tranquility, as they were invaded by the giants called Ronnongwetowanea, who came from the north and inhabited considerably; but their mode of attack was slily, and never dared to precipitate themselves upon the enemy without prospect of success; especially they took advantage when the warriors were absent from the town. After plundering the people's houses and making captives those who were found, and hastily retreat to their residence in the north. An instance—a family of princes lived near the river St. Lawrence, of whom, containing six brothers and a sister and their father, was a noble chieftain, who fell at the contest of the enemy. One time the brothers went out a day's hunt and leaving their sister alone in the camp; unfortunately while they were gone the giant makes vigorous attacks and the woman soon became a prey to the invaders. On the eve the brothers returned and were much

10

grieved that their sister was found missing; they immediately made a search, but the night was getting too late, and the darkness prevented them. On the morning the eldest brother determined to pursue the enemy until he could discover something about their sister, and promised to return in seven days if nothing should happen, accordingly the prince set out and pursued the traces of the enemy; after journeyed three days he reached the giant's residence about sundown; at first sight he discovered his sister was gathering some sticks for fuel near the house; but as he approached the sister retired; the princess soon proved by her conduct that she had fell in love with the giant, and that it was impossible to gain her confidence. The prince was now brought to a point of view about the dread of the enemy; but however he was willing to risk the dangers he was about to meet; he remained until about dusk and then entered the house; happily he was received with most favorable terms, and his fears were soon dissipated, the giant offered his pipe as a tribute of respect, which the prince accepted. After receiving the evening diet they talked a good while without a least appearance of hostility; as the night was getting late the prince was invited to a bed; but the giant was now acting to deceive the prince; he commenced to amuse him part of the night in sing-

11

ing songs; the giant had determined to assassinate the visiter the first opportunity as the prince was so fatigued that he was now fast asleep; he killed him on the bed and the body was deposited in a cave near the house where he had stored the carcasses. The giant was much pleased of his conquest over the prince, he advised his wife to watch daily in order to impose on another enemy. The seven days elapsed, as the brother did not return the youngest brother Donhtonha was much excited about his brother and resolved to pursue him; the Donhtonha was the most stoutest and ferocious looking fellow, after arming himself commenced the journey, and also arrived at the place and time as mentioned, and found his sister; but before he had time to reconcile her she returned to the house as she had formerly done, and informed the giant that some person was coming: the Donhtonha entered the house with appearances of hostile disposition, and enquired for his brother; this produced alarm: the giant was promptly to pacify the prince: he replied that he had made peace with the brother, who had gone to visit some people in the neighborhood, and it was expected he would return every moment. Upon this assurance the Donhtonha became some abated; the sister provided some food and he soon enjoyed the domestic felicity: but, alas, the giant was far from being friendly and was only forming a plan to deceive the visiter. The evening was late, the Donhtonha was out of patience waiting for his brother to come home, and renewed his enquiries; the visitor was invited to bed; the giant was in hopes to exterminate the visiter: he rose from his seat and commenced his usual custom in singing. The Donhtonha perceived that some evil design was performing against him and resolved to abandon the bed for awhile; he begged leave for a few moments and went out after various considerations from being imposed; he procured some pieces of wood which produced a faint light in the night and put it above his eyelids and again went to bed; the giant was now deceived; while the visiter was asleep his eyes appeared as though he was awake continually. As soon as day light the visiter hurried from the bed, and was about to make a search for the deceased brother, but the giant protested which soon excited suspicions of the act: after a long debate the Donhtonha attacked the giant: a severe conflict ensued, at last the giant was killed; and burnt him in the ruins of his house, but his spirit fled to heaven and changed into one of the eastern stars. During the engagement his sister was grieved and fled to the wilderness, and lamented for her deceased husband, and she died

13

in despair, and her spirit also became one of the northern stars. After the conquest the search was prosecuted, he discoved the remains of his brother and weeps over it and burnt it to ashes.

At a time another Ronnongwetowanea attacked a small town located on the bank of the Kanawage, (St. Lawrence.) This occurred in a season when the people were out to hunt, and there was no person in the town except an old chief and an attendant named Yatatonwatea: while they were enjoying repose in their houses were suddenly attacked by the Ronnongwetowanea: but the Yatatonwatea escaped, went out the back door and deserted the aged chief to the fate: however the enemy spared no time, the chase was soon prosecuted which caused the Yatatonatea to retreat as fast as possible; he attempted to make resistance in various places, but was compelled to retire at the appearance of the enemy; in vain he endeavored to gain retreat by traversing various creeks and hills: he undertook a new method of giving little effect upon the progress of the enemy; after running some distance he discovered which would promptly cherish the imposition, he drove a flock of pigeons in the way to amuse the (giant) until he could hide himself under the bank of the river, unfortunately the flattering hope seemed to fail:

14

after remaining there but a short time before he saw the enemy was coming in full speed, and was soon obliged to abandon the position and continue the flight: again he tried to conceal himself among the rocks of the mountains, but in a mean time the enemy advanced at the moment, of which he became dismayed, finding that nothing could resist the impetuosity of the pursuer, but determined not to surrender as long as he was capable to keep out of the reach; he immediately took the path which leads to the hunting grounds in search of some people fortunately at a short distance met two warriors and he was instantly supported and made vigorous resistance; after terrible combat the Ronnongwetowanea was exterminated: during the time the warriors conducted themselves as heroes, which gained the triumph, notwithstanding one of them received a severe wound by the club. The Yatatonwatea with alarm whoop hastened to the encampment and advised the people of the substance and the dangers which the enemy might commit upon the vacant towns. As soon as the people received the intelligence immediately returned to their settlements, and a convention were held by the chieftain in order to take some measures to defend their country. As the Ronnongwetowanea tribe were not numerous and deemed it expedient to raise a large force and therefore a few hundred warriors were sent to subdue them: after decisive contests the warriors gained the victory: and it was supposed that the Ronnongwetowanea tribe has ever since ceased to exist. (This fate

1000 B.C. happened probably about two thousand five hundred winters before Columbus discovered the America.) The depredations of the enemy which so often exercised upon the inhabitants were now terminated: and the country enjoyed without disturbance many winters. About this time a mischievous person named Shotyerronsgwea, while visiting the people at first distinguished himself of a good character and in mean time gained the confidence of the people: by doing this he was fairly concealed from being discovered of his real designs, and in a short time began to injure the people: he assassinated two warriors secretly, and then violated six virgins, etc. And the next he ventured to break the harmony of the nation and created dissensions among the people. At this the chiefs were so offended that the Shotyeronsgwea was banished from the village: when he received this treatment he deemed proper to desist from going back to any of the towns: he immediately crossed the river St. Lawrence and move toward the mid-day sun, and he came to a town situated south of the great

16

lake (Ontario) and he was received with kindness; but his entertainment could not appease his evil designs; though he appeared reconciled, one night while at the dancing house he killed several warriors; this offence he discovered should prove fatal to his person, and was compelled to leave the town and went some other place to do mischief. The Shotyeronagwea was the greatest mischievous person that ever existed on the continent. He was considered an agent from bad spirit. About this time Big Quisquiss (perhaps the Mammoth) invaded the settlements south of Ontario lake: the furious animal push down the houses and made a great disturbance: the people was compelled to flee from the terrible monster: the warriors made opposition but failed; at length a certain chief warrior collected the men from several towns—a severe engagement took place, at last the monster retired, but the people could not remain long without being disturbed: Big Elk invaded the towns: the animal was furious and destroyed many persons: however the men were soon collected—a severe contest ensued and the monster was killed.

About this time the northern nations formed a confederacy and seated a great council fire on river St. Lawrence; the northern nations possessed the bank of the great lakes: the countries in the north were plenty of beavers, but the hunters were often opposed by the big snakes. The people live on the south side of the Big Lakes make bread of roots and obtain a kind of potatoes and beans found on the rich soil.

Perhaps about two thousand two hundred years before the Columbus discovered the America, and northern nations appointed a prince, and immediately repaired to the south and visited the great Emperor who resided at the Golden City, a capital of the vast empire.

700 B.C.

After a time the Emperor built many forts throughout his dominions and almost penetrated the lake Erie; this produced an excitement, the people of the north felt that they would soon be deprived of the country on the south side of the Great Lakes they determined to defend their country against any infringement of foreign people: long bloody wars ensued which perhaps lasted about one hundred years; the people of the north were too skillful in the use of bows and arrows and could endure hardships which proved fatal to a foreign people; at last the northern nations gained the conquest and all the towns and forts were totally destroyed and left them in the heap of ruins.

About this time a great horned serpent appeared on lake Ontario, the serpent produced diseases and

18

many of the people died, but by the aid of thunder bolts the monster was compelled to retire. A blazing star fell into a fort situated on the St. Lawrence and destroyed the people; this event was considered as a warning of their destruction. After a time a war broke out among the northern nations which continued until they had utterly destroyed each other, the island again become in possession of fierce animals.

PART III.

Origin of the Kingdom of the Five Nations, which was called a Long House: the Wars, Fierce Animals, etc.

By some inducement a body of people was concealed in the mountain at the falls named Kuskehsawkich, (now Oswego.) *A.D. 1* When the people were released from the mountain they were visited by *Tarenyawagon,* i.e. the Holder of the Heavens, who had power to change himself into various shapes; he ordered the people to proceed towards the sunrise as he guided them and come to a river and named Yenonanatche, i.e. going round a mountain, (now Mohawk,) and went down the bank of the river and come to where it discharges into a great river running towards the midday sun: and Shaw-nay-taw-ty, i.e. beyond the Pineries, (now Hudson,) and went down the bank of the river and touched bank of a great water. The company made encampment at the place and remained there a few days. The people were yet in one language: some of the people went to the banks of the great water towards the midday sun; but the main company returned as they came, on the bank of the river, under the direction of the holder of the Heavens. Of this company there was a particular body which called themselves one houset hold; of these were six families and they entered into a resolution to preserve the chain of alliance which should not be extinguished in any manner. The company advanced some distance up the river of Shaw-na-taw-ty, (Hudson) the Holder of the Heavens directs the first family to make their residence near the bank of the river, and the family was named Te-haw-re-hogeh, i.e. a speech divided, (now Mohawk) and their language was soon altered; the company then turned and went towards the sunsetting, and travelled about two days and a half and come to a creek,* which was named Kaw-na-taw-te-ruh. i.e. Pineries. The second family was directed to make their residence near the creek, and the family was named Ne-haw-re-tah-go. i.e. Big Tree, now Oneidas, and likewise their language was altered. The company continued to proceed towards the sunsetting: under the direction of the Holder of the Heavens. The third family was directed to make their residence on a mountain named Onondaga (now Onondaga) and the family was named Seuh-now-kah-tah. i.e. carrying the name, and their language was altered. The com-

---

* The creek now branches off the Susquehanna River at the head generally called Col. Allen's lake, ten miles south of Oneida castle.

pany continued their journey towards the sunsetting. The fourth family was directed to make their residence near a long lake named Go-yo-goh, i.e. a mountain rising from water, (now Cayuga) and the family was named Sho-nea-na-we-to-wah. i.e. a great pipe, their language was altered. The company continued to proceed towards the sunsetting. The fifth family was directed to make their residence near a high mountain, or rather nole, situated south of the Canandaigua lake. which was named Jenneatowake and the family was named Te-how-nea-nyo-hent, i. e. Possessing a Door, now Seneca and their language was altered. The sixth family went with the company that journeyed towards the sunsetting, and touched the bank of a great lake, and named Kau-ha-gwa-rah-ka, i.e. A Cap, now Erie, and then went towards between the mid-day and sunsetting, and travelled considerable distance and come to a large river which was named Ouau-we-yo-ka, i.e. a principal stream, now Mississippi; the people discovered a grape vine lying across the river by which a part of the people went over,* but while they were engaged, the vine broke, and were divided, they became enemies to those who went over the river; in consequence they were obliged to

---

* By Some this may seem an incredible story. Why more so than that the Israelites should cross the Red Sea on dry land.

23

dispense the journey. The Holder of the Heavens instruct them in the art of bows and arrows in the time of game and danger. Associates are dispersed, and each family went to search for residences according to their conveniences of game. The sixth family went towards the sunnse and touched the bank of the great water. The family was directed to make their residence near Cau-ta-noh, i.e. Pine in water, situated near the mouth of the Nuse river, now in North Carolina, and the family was named Kau-ta-noh, now Tuscarora and their language was also altered: but the six families did not go so far as to loose the understanding of each others language. The Holder of the Heavens returns to the five families and forms the mode of confederacy which was named Ggo-nea-seab-neh i.e. A Long House, to which are 1st—Tea-kaw-reh-ho-geh; 2d—New-haw-teh-tah-go; 3d—Seuh-nau-ka-ta; 4th—Sho-nea-na-we-to-wan; 5th—Te-hoo-nea-nyo-hent. About this time it is supposed an agent from superior power solemnly visits the families, and he instructs them in various things respecting the infinity, matrimony, moral rules, worship, etc.; and he warns them that an evil spirit was in the world and would induce the people to commit trespasses against the rules he had given them: and he offers them favorable promises of obedience to rules, the souls would enter the place of happiness; but to the disobedient their souls would be sent to a state of misery. And he gives the seeds for corn, beans, squashes, potatoes and tobacco, with directions how to cultivate them; and he gives them the dogs to aid in pursuing the game; and he repeats the administration of the game; and that the great country was given for their people's maintenance. When he ended the interview of consolation he leaves.

About one hundred winters since the people left the mountain,—the five families were increased and made some villages in the country. The Holder of the Heavens was absent from the country, which was destitute of the visits of the Governor of the Universe. The reason produced the occasion that they were invaded by the monsters called Ko-nea-rau-neh-neh, i.e. Flying Heads, which devoured several people of the country. The Flying Heads made invasions in the night; but the people were attentive to escape by leaving their huts and concealing themselves in other huts prepared for that purpose. An instance:—there was an old woman which resided at Onondaga; she was left alone in the hut at evening, while others deserted. She was setting near the fire parching some acorns when the

A.D.
100

25

monstrous Head made its appearance at the door; while viewing the woman it was amazed that she eat the coals of fire, by which the monsters were put to flight, and ever since the heads disappeared and were supposed concealed in the earth. After a short time the people were invaded by the monster of the deep; the Lake Serpent traverses the country, which interrupted their intercourse. The five families were compelled to make fortifications throughout their respective towns, in order to secure themselves from the devouring monsters. The manner of making the fort: at first they set fire against several trees as requires to make a fort, and the stone axes are used to rub off the coals, as to burn quicker; when the tree burns down they put fires to it about three paces apart and burns it down in half a day; the logs are collected to a place where they set up round according to the bigness of the fort, and the earth is heaped on both sides. A fort generally has two gates; one for passage, and the other to obtain water. The people had implements which they used to make bow and arrows. The kettle is made of baked clay in which the meat is boiled; the awl and needles are made of hard bone; a pipe for smoking, is made of baked clay, or soft stone; a small turtle shell is used to peel the bark; a small dry stick is used to make a fire, by boring it against the seasoned wood.

Perhaps about 1250 years before Columbus discovered the America, about two hundred and fifty winters since the people left the mountain, the five families *A.D. 250* became numerous and extended their settlements, as the country had been exposed to the invasion of the monsters, that the people could not enjoy but a short space of time without being molested. About this time a powerful tribe of the wilderness, called Ot-ne-yar-heh, i.e. Stonish Giants* overrun the country and the warriors were immediately collected from several towns and a severe combat took place, but the warriors were overpowered and the people fell at the mercy of the invaders, and the people were threatened with destruction, and the country was brought to subjection for many winters. As he people have been reduced so often they could not increase. The Stonish Giants were so ravenous that they devoured the people

---

* It appears by the traditions of the Shawnees that the Stonish Giants descend from a certain family that journeyed on the east side of Mississippi River, went towards the northwest after they were separated, on account of the vine broke. The family was left to seek its habitation, and the rules of humanity were forgotten, and afterwards eat raw flesh of the animals. At length they practiced rolling themselves on the sand, by means their bodies were covered with hard skin these people became giants and were dreadful invaders of the country. It is said that Sir William Johnson, the Superintendents of the Six Nations, had a picture of the giant. Probably the English have recorded in the Historian respecting North America.

of almost every town in the country; but happily
the Holder of the Heavens again visits the people
and he observes that the people were in distressed
condition on the account of the enemy. With a
stratagem he proceeds to banish their invaders,
and he changes himself into a giant, and combines
the Stonish Giants, he introduces them to take the
lead to destroy the people of the country; but a
day's march they did not reach the fort Onondaga,
where they intended to invade, and he ordered
them to lay in a deep hollow* during the night and
they would make attack on the following morning.
At the dawn of the day, the Holder of the Heavens
ascended upon the heights and he overwhelms
them by a mass of rocks, and only one escaped to
announce the dreadful fate: and since the event the
Stonish Giants left the country and seeks an asy-
lum in the regions of the north. The families were
now preserved from extinction. The Lake Serpent
discovers the powerful operations of the Holder of
the Heavens, instantly retreats into the deep places
of the lakes. After the banishment of the monster
of the deep made its appearance in the country: a
snake with the shape of human head opposed the
passage between the Onondaga and Go-yo-gouh,

* The hollow it is said not far from Onondaga. Some says the Giants
retreated by way of Mountain Ridge and crossed below Niagara
Falls.

now Cayuga, which prevented their intercourse, as the snake had seated near the principal path leads through the settlement of the Five Families. The people were troubled of their condition, and finally they determined to make resistance. They selected the best warriors at Onondaga and after they were organized and prepared proceeded to the place: after a severe conflict the snake was killed: the lake serpent was often seen by the people, but the thunder bolt destroyed the serpent or compelled them to retire into the deep. About this time they were various nations inhabited the southern countries, these nations descended from the families that were dispersed after the vine broke on Onauweyoka, (Mississippi). The Holder of the Heavens visited the Five Families and instructed them in the arts of war, and favors them to gain the country beyound their limits, after which he disappeared.

Perhaps 1,000 years before Columbus discovered the America.—About this time the Five Families become independent *A.D. 500* nations, and they formed a council fire in each nation, etc. Unfortunately a war broke out among the Five Nations; during the unhappy differences the Atotarho was the most hostile chief, resided at the fort Onondaga: his head and body

29

was ornamented with black snakes:—his dishes and spoons were made of skulls of the enemy: after a while he requested the people to change his dress, the people immediately drove away the snakes—a mass of wampam were collected and the chief was soon dressed in a large belt of wampam; he become a law giver and renewed the chain of alliance of the Five Nations and framed their internal government, which took five years in accomplishing it. At Onondaga a tree of peace was planted reached the clouds of Heaven; under the shade of this tree the Senators are invited to set and delilerate, and smoke the pipe of peace as ratification of their proceedings; a great council fire was kindled under the majestic tree, having four branches, one pointed to the south, west, east, north: the neighboring nations were amazed at the powerful confederates: the Onondaga was considered a heart of the country: numerous belts and strings of wampam were left with the famous chief as record of alliance, etc., after he had accomplished the noble work he was immediately named Atotarho, King of the Five nations: and was governed by the Senate, chosen by the people annually; the successor of the kings to follow the woman's line. About this time the Te-hoo-nea-nyo-hent, or Senecas, was at war with the Squawkeihows, a powerful tribe past the banks of the Genesee river: after various engagements the Senecas sent an army to scourge the enemy, but were repulsed with a severe loss; the melancholy intelligence was soon conveyed to Onondaga and informed the king of their defeat: a powerful army of the allies were soon directed against the Squawkihows; after a long seige the principal fort was surrendered without discretion, and the chief was taken prisoner, put to death, the war terminated, however a remnant of the Squawkeihows were allowed to remain in the country and became vassals to the five nations after the conquest. The government ordered the Senecas to settle the country and to build forts on the Genesee River, as to keep Squawkhaws in subjection, for fearing in time they might create a rebellion. The Senecas now possessed along the bank of the Great Lake, now Ontario, to the creek called Kenaukarent, now Oak Orchard, the bank of the river Onyakarra, now Niagara, possessed by Twakanhah, (Mississaugers.)

In the days the king Atotarho II, about this time the Oyalquoher or big bear invaded the territory of the five nations, the hunters were often attacked by these monsters. At the village of Ohiokea, situated west of Oneida creek, a small party went out to hunt and encamped near the lake Skonyatales; one

morning while they were in the camp a noise broke
out in the lake; a man was sent immediately to see
the tumult: he saw a great bear on the bank rolling down stones and logs: the monster appeared
to be in a great rage: a lion came out of the lake
and suddenly fell upon the bear, a severe contest
ensued, in the mean time the bear was beaten and
was compelled to leave the bank, the next day the
men went in search of the bear: they found the
bear: one of the fore legs was so heavy that two
men could not lift but a hands high, they procured
some of the meat for useful purposes in the time
of war. About this time a great musqueto invaded
the fort Onondaga: the musqueto was mischievous
to the people, it flew about the fort with a long
stinger, and sucked the blood a number of lives;
the warriors made several oppositions to expel the
monster, but failed; the country was invaded until
the Holder of the Heavens was pleased to visit
the people: while he was visiting the king at the
fort Onondaga, the musqueto made appearance as
usual and flew about the fort, the Holder of the
Heavens attacked the monster, it flew so rapidly
that he could hardly keep in sight of it, but after
a few days chase the monster began to fail; he
chased on the borders of the great lakes towards
the sunsetting, and round the great country: at last

he overtook the monster and kill it near the salt lake Onondaga and the blood became small musquetos.

In the reign the king Atotarho III. About this time the Oneidas had extended their forts down the river Kaunsehwatauyea, or Susquehanna, a fort situated on the river there was a certain woman delivered a male child uncommon size; when he was twelve years of age he was nearly as large as grown person, and he would beat his playmates which would create disputes, but the mother would correct him, and afterward she prevailed, he promised never to injure his people: when grown up he became a giant and was a great hunter: the parent was stored with venison continually: he was so strong that when returned from hunting he would have five or six deers and bears strung around on his belt. The giant was named Soh-nou-re-wah, i.e. Big Neck, (now Shawnees) which inhabited the banks of the river and brought several suits of dress and the scalps of whom he had killed. The Sau-wau-noo sends messengers to fort Kau-na-sen-wa-tau-yea as to demonstrate the conduct of Soh-nau-ro-wah, but the business was left upon the relatives Sau-rau-ra-wah, who persuaded him to reform his behavior for the future: he remained only two winters without making disturbance: he went down the river and whenever he came to a town he committed the same outrages upon the inhabitants and plundered the people's clothes, skins, etc. Again the Sau-wa-noo sends a deputy and reported their resentment, but determined to make hostile aggressions if not satisfaction was made on their part. The chief Ne-nau-re-tah-go sends a belt of wampum and offered the terms of peace which was accepted, but the Sau-rau-roh-wah was not disposed to favor the treaty; he left the fort and went down and located on the bank of Kau-nau-seh-wah-tau-yea river, (said Susque-hanna,) and commenced to build a fort*; he was frequently visited by his relatives: and after the fortification was completed he resolved to continue the war against his enemies: he went from time to time and attacked the people which inhabited on the river as he had done before; he would lay in ambush near the path, and whenever the people are passing he shoots them; he used a plump arrow, which was so body in two parts: as he became mischievous to the people that the relatives were obliged to form a plan to destroy him, but Sah-nou-ro-wah was pleased of the visit and the food which was given; but while he was eating

---

* The fort was situated on the south bank of the Susquehanna river. In 1800 I went over the ground myself and viewed the mound.

it one of the warriors, with a club concealed under his cloak, instantly stepped on the bench where he was sitting, and gave a fatal blow on the monster's head, he was so distracted that he ran out of the fort and was intended to cross the river, he sunk in the mire which was near the bank, the warriors prevailed and killed him on the spot; the warriors spoiled his house and obtained a large quantity of skins, etc.: and the fort was ruined ever since.

Perhaps about 800 years before the Columbus discovered America. About this time the Twakanhahors, (now Mississaugers,) *A.D. 700* ceded the colonies lying between the Kea-nau-hau sent (Oak Orchard,) and the river Onyakarra, (Niagara) to the Five Nations.

About this time lived the king Atotarho IIII. There was a woman and son resided near the fort which was situated near a nole, which was named Jenneatowaka, the original seat of the Te-hoo-nea-nyo-hent (Senecas,) the boy one day while amusing in the bush he caught a small serpent called Kaistowanea, with two heads, and brings it to his apartment; the serpent was first placed in a small bark box to tame, which was fed with birds, flesh, etc. After ten winters the serpent became considerable large and rested on the beams within the hut, and the warrior was obliged to hunt deers and

35

bears to feed the monster; but after awhile the serpent was able to maintain itself on various game; it left the hut and resided on the top of a nole: the serpent frequently visited the lake, and after thirty years it was prodigious size, which in a short time inspired with an evil mind against the people, and in the night the warrior experienced the serpent was brooding some mischief, and was about to destroy the people of the fort; when the warrior was acquainted of the danger he was dismayed and soon moved to other fort; at daylight the serpent descended from the heights with the most tremendous noise of the trees, which were trampled down in such a force that the trees were uprooted, and the serpent immediately surrounded the gate; the people were taken improvidentially and brought to confusion; finding themselves circled by the monstrous serpent, some of them endeavored to pass out at the gate, and others attempted to climb over the serpent, but were unable; the people remained in this situation for several days; the warriors had made oppositions to dispel the monster, but were fruitless, and the people were distressed of their confinement, and found no other method than to rush to pass out at the gate, but the people were devoured, except a young warrior and sister, which detained and were only left exposed to the mon-

ster, and were restrained without hopes of getting
released: at length the warrior received advice
from a dream, and he adorned his arms with the
hairs of his sister, which he succeeded by shoot-
ing at the heart, and the serpent was mortally
wounded, which hastened to retire from the fort
and retreated to the lake in order to gain relief; the
serpent dashed on the face of the water furiously in
the time of agony; at last it vomited the substance
which it had eaten and then sunk to the deep and
expired. The people of the fort did not receive any
assistance from their neighboring forts as the serpent was too powerful to be resisted. After the fort
was demolished the Council fire was removed to
other fort called Thau-gwe-took, which was situated west of now, Geneva Lake, erected bulwarks
on Mountain Ridge west of Genesee River.

About this time reigned the King Atotarho IV.
At the fort Ke-dau-yer-ka-wau (now Tonewanta
plains) a party went out to hunt and were attacked
by the Ot-tau-wahs, which created differences
between the two nations as they entered on no
terms but to commence hostilities: to To-hoo-nyo-
hent sends a band of warriors to attack some of
the hunters as to retaliate the vengeance upon their
enemies. The warriors advanced above the lake
named Geattahgweah (now Chautauque) and made

encampment and agreed to hunt two days, after which to proceed toward the enemies' country: the warriors went in various directions: a certain warrior passed a small brook, he discovered a strange animal resembling a dog, but could not discover the head, the creature was a greyish color, and was laying asleep exposed to the rays of the sun: and also discovered a den supposed the place of this residence: the warrior returned to the camp at evening and related the kind of animal, and informed them as he imagined was a very poisonous animal, and he was afraid to approach it again, but one of the jokers laughed at him and he was called a cowardly fellow: the joker determined to go himself and kill the creature without trouble, but wished some of the warriors to be spectators in the time of the engagement: accordingly the warrior went, accompanied by a number of warriors: he was directed to the spot and discovered the animal. After beating it short time with his club, he seized the animal and tied it with a tum line: but while he was lifting it the creature immediately moved to the den. With all his might he held the tum line, but he could not stop it, he was compelled to let go the tum line when the creature went beyond his reach; the warrior was confused at not being able to kill the animal: he hastened to retire from the

spot, but when a few paces he was taken with the
pestilence which was influenced by the creature,
and suddenly died; another warrior was at sight
and directly fled to carry the intelligence, but also
died a short distance, and the others returned to the
camp; but the pestilence soon prevailed among the
warriors, and many of them died in the same manner: a few of them escaped by leaving the camp
before the plague appeared, and thus ended the
expedition. The Ottauwahs continued their hostilities and attacked the hunters: the Senecas sent out
a small party and fought—drove the enemy off, but
their engagements were small and continued many
winters.

In the days of king Ototarho VI, perhaps
650 years before the Columbus discovered the America, at the fort
Keadanyeekowa or Tontawanta plains,
a small party went out to make incursion upon the
enemy that may be found within the boundaries of
the kingdom. They penetrated the Ohio river and
encamped on the bank: as they were out of provi-
sion, the warriors were anxious to kill a game; a
certain warrior discovered a hollow tree, suppos-
ing a bear in the tree, he immediately reported: the
warriors were in hopes to obtain the bear—went to
the tree; one of them climbed and put a fire in it in

A.D. 850

order to drive out the creature: the warriors made ready to shoot, but were mistaken, there instantly came out a furious Lizard, and quickly grasped and leaped into the hollow of the tree and the young ones devoured it: a grumbling noise ensued, the warriors were terrified at the monstrous creature and were soon compelled to retire, except one staid at the tree while others fled: he remained until the party was destroyed and the last warrior was chased; the warrior immediately left the tree and ran on the way fortunately met the Holder of the Heavens who advised him to stop and offers the aid of material resistance which was accepted: the warrior was instructed to make fire without delay and to get some sticks to use with which to prevent the Lizard's flesh from uniting the body or being efficatious, the protector changed into a lion and laid in wait, in a meanwhile the monster came up, a severe engagement took place, the warrior hastened with a stick and began to hook the Lizard's flesh, when bit off by his defendant and throws it into the fire, by means the monster was quelled. The warrior thanked for the personal preservation. The protector vanished out of his sight. The warrior returned to the fort and related the occurrence. The war raged; the Senecas had sent out parties against the Ottauwahs and obtained various successes; at last the Ottauwahs sued for peace. After a few winters the Senecas gained their mutual intercourse with the Ottauwahs and other neighboring nations.

About this time reigned the king Ototarho VII, who authorized by the Senate to send an expedition to explore the countries towards the setting sun, he sends a messenger to acquaint the Ottauwahs of his intention, and wished them to form such arrangements and to favor their passage, which was complied agreeable to his request. The king appointed two captains to command the expedition, about fifteen men were selected from the five nations: after they were equiped and prepared, commenced the journey and arrived at Sandusky; the King of Ottauwahs sent two warriors to accompany the expedition; on their way held several conferences with the nations and all seemed to favor their passage. They advanced the Mississippi river, a duke of Twa-kan-ah had collected the people from several towns, came out to meet them the people around them, singing, beating their little drums; after danced the ceremony was performed the band of warriors was invited into the national house. The band crossed the Mississippi and continued their course towards the sunsetting; they reached an extensive meadow: they discovered a curious animal—a winged fish, it flew about the tree; this little active creature moved like a humming bird. They continued the journey and come at the village of the Dog Tail Nation, the band was accommodated, amused with dances, and was conducted to the chief's house. They were astonished that the people had short tails like apes; a hole was made through their seats where they put their tails. The band continued their direction and come to another nation and too was kindly received, and their object was favorably accepted by the head men of the nation. During their stay, a certain warrior of the band courted a young woman, but the warrior died soon after the marriage. They observed that the people did not eat any meat but drink the soup. The band continued the journey, but before reaching the Rocky Mountains were arrested by a giant; the band was compelled to return; after a long journey came back to the seat and informed the king all the particulars about the journey. After a time the five nations was desirous to preserve the peace and friendship with the western nations; ambassador was sent to the Lentahkeh nation, who inhabited the country east of Ohio River (now in Kentucky); another ambassador was sent who went and lived among the Ottauwahs for several years; he married a woman and afterward obtained two children; he was invited to join a company going out a winter's hunt. They journeyed some distance, and reached their hunting grounds; but the men were so unlucky that they could kill but a few game; after a few days the people were destitute of provisions; the leader of the company commanded the overseer to select two fat persons and to kill them without delay, which was soon executed; the flesh of these victims was distributed among the people. The leader had commanded the people that if any one had killed a game the meat should be left with the overseer for distribution, and that who disobeyed, the offender should be punished in a severest manner. The ambassy killed a bear, the meat was disposed to the rules. The leader daily butchered two persons to feed the people, which only increased their distress. The people were so feeble that they were unable to hunt any more, and many of them began to famish. The ambassy again killed another game and bring it secretly to his camp, but it was soon detected and rumored among the people; at this offense the ambassy was ordered to appear before their tribunal; some men were angry at him and sought to destroy him, but the leader deemed it unjust, it would violate the treaty they had entered with the five nations; but however, to satisfy the people, the leader consented to use other method to destroy him; he commanded to strip him and to seize his clothes and the instruments; after which to extinguish their fires, and then to remove their camp a half day's journey distance; the offender would certainly freeze without remedy; but the ambassy was ingenious, finding that he would be surprised, instantly takes a suit of dress and bow and arrows, and hides them under the hemlock boughs which were spread in the camp. In a meanwhile the opponents entered the camp, the ambassy was stripped without discriminate as they had determined to destroy him. The wife was compelled to leave him, or else she would share the same fate.

The company retired: he dressed himself immediately and proceeded and was in hopes to reach a fort situated near the Lake Erie: but was so fatigued that he could not travel very fast: about sunset he happened to approach on an age of a dark forest: he selected a spot where he encamped, but as he had no kind of food to eat and was quite dejected after making exertions to make himself comfortable, but failed, the weather being unfavorable, as it was cold and cloudy, however, he was seldom taken by surprise: having a good understanding about astronomical calculations, ascertained that the storm was at hand: after kindled a fire laid himself down to linger out a miserable existence which he was doomed to suffer. Early in the morning he heard some noise as something was coming, which at once attracted his attention: he was afraid: as presumed that some of his enemy had overtook him: fortunately a young man came up and sat down: the visitor showed a friendly disposition, after a short conversation the ambassy related his distressed condition: the visitor offered to relieve him as soon as possible, which was received with sanguine expectations: the ambassy was advised that a snow would fall so deep that he would be in want of a pair of snow shoes, the visitor offered the pattern, and showed him how to make the shoes. The ambassy was directed where to find the game: and did as he was bidden. On the night the young man made another visit and advised the ambassy where to catch bears: after the conversation the visitor disappeared. He succeeded and caught seven bears: after he had prepared some meat and the bears' oil, immediately went to the encampment in search of his wife and children, found them almost perished; at first gave them each a spoonful of oil and were soon relieved: he directed them to his camp. The ambassy was relieved from distress whilst his enemy was lingering in despair: he examined the camp and was astonished to find that the people were utterly famished: the people became so weak and faint that they were not able to make fire: those who held out had eat the human flesh as long as they could they themselves, and were lying among the dead, the company was now exposed to destruction, as the people had put themselves to disgrace: the ambassy had refused to invite any of them except his wife's relatives: the disisters were so worn out did not reach the camp until next morning. After a few days by his exertions, the men's strength was revived, and were capable to hunt. After they had come back to the town the ambassy was so shamefully abused by the people he was compelled to leave his wife and the country. About this time the Ottauwahs became numerous and powerful nation, occupied an extensive country lying between the Lake Erie and the Ohio river, and was supposed their national force amounted to about 4000 men.

In the reign of King Atotarho VIII perhaps 400 years before the Columbus discovered America.

About this time the Twakanhah or *A.D. 1100* Messissaugers began to wage a war against the five nations: the Senecas on the frontier were most engaged in the warfare. After various skirmishes the enemy was so excited that they determined to destroy the fort

46

Kauhanauka (now in Tuscarora near Lewiston,) but the commander of the fort was aware of the danger, he sent messengers to the forts in the vicinity, and about eight hundred warriors were collected at fort Kauhanauka. The commander had sent runners to observe the movements of the enemy. The army marched towards the river, and hid themselves among the bushes under the mountain: the enemy came up: a bloody battle ensued: the enemy was repulsed and flies from the foe. The army returned to the fort; soon after the commander dispatched two runners to the forts on the Genesee river to procure assistance as soon as possible; the army received reinforcements; they made bark canoes and carried them to the mouth of the Niagara river; the canoes were ready, the commander sent a chieftain and offered the enemy an intermission or parley, but the proposal was not accepted; the army immediately crossed the river and made vigorous attack: the enemy was routed and fled from the bank without making resistance, retreated towards the head of the lake; after burning the huts, the army returned to the fort; but the commotions were not quelled; small parties of the Senecas often take the canoes and go by water towards the head of Ontario lake, in search of the enemy, but they avoid from attack of superior force; several

47

engagements were made on the lake with small parties of the enemy; after a while the commander of the fort Kauhanauka, was ardent to attack the main body of the enemy: he sends runners beyond the Genesee river, and obtained two thousand warriors; the army again crossed the Niagara river and proceeded towards the head of the lake, but before reached the beach met a strong force of the enemy; after a desperate contest the army retreated; the commander soon perceived that it was impossible to gain the conquest, sued for peace and offered to restore the prisoners which he took from them which was concluded. About this time the Stonish Giants were diminished, but very few found in the north regions; the Giants understood the language of the five nations, but they were a most savage tribe, and often attacked the hunters, but that set of hordes were extirpated. At the Onondaga two men went out to hunt beaver, and crossed the river St. Lawrence, and went far in the north, and discovered a number of beaver dams, and killed many beavers. One day a man went alone in search of the beaver, but unfortunately he was taken prisoner by the Stonish Giant: the man was compelled to run a race with the giant, a considerable distance; after midday the man gained and almost went out of sight, but the giant whooped, by which the man

48

was so affected that he fainted and fell down. The giant took advantage of him and soon passed him; the man was dismayed and turned his course, and sought to escape and endeavored to hide himself: he climbed a small tree and bent it to another tree, and leaped from tree to tree, until he reached a large basswood stump which had sprouted several branches, and seated himself in the midst of it and watched the pursuer: in a few moments the giant came up and examined the stump for some time; at length the giant exhibited a curious instrument, which he called a pointer, and possessed a power of the nature; it directed him where to find game; the giant could not live without it. The man observed the motion of the hand, and as it was about to point to him, he jumped from the stump and seized it by the fingers, and instantly possessed the valuable instrument; the giant was defeated and immediately entreated for the pointer, and offered to mention the medical roots as a mark of friendship, which was accepted; the pointer was restored to the owner, after which the giant retired; the man came home and began to doctor, and cured many diseases; he was skilled in the business and drew hair and worms from the persons whom the witches had blown into their bodies. It was supposed that the Skauniatohatihawk, or Nantcokes in the south first founded the witchcraft. Great pains were taken to procure the snakes and roots which the stuff was made of to poison the people. The witches formed into a secret society: they met in the night and consult on various subject respecting their engagements; when a person becomes a member of their society, he is forbidden to reveal any of their proceedings. The witches in the night could turn into foxes and wolves, and run very swift, attending with flashes of light. The witches sometimes turned into a turkey or big owl, and can fly very fast, and go from town to town, and blow hairs and worms into a person; if the witches are discovered by some person they turn into a stone or rotten log; in this situation they are entirely concealed; about fifty persons were indicted for being witches, and were burnt to death near the fort Onondaga, by order of the national committee. About this time a strange thing happened near the village of Kaunehsuntahkeh, situated east of Oneida creek: a man and his wife and another person returned from hunting, but before they reached the village the night was getting late; they went into a house to stay over the night; the house where the dead bodies were deposited; they kindled a fire and went to sleep, but when the fire was out, the room became dark, the man heard something was gnawing: the man kindled the fire, he discovered the person was dead eaten by a ghost; he was so frightened that he trembled; he immediately told his wife to quit the room as soon as possible; he remained a few moments and also left the house and followed his wife and overtook her, but she became faint and could not run fast; they saw a light coming and supposed the ghost was chasing; fortunately they gained the village. The next day the people went and burnt the dead bodies. This important event was soon made known among the five nations, and afterward changed their mode of burying, by setting posture face to the east; but again they were troubled with the dead bodies, and were compelled to make some alterations in burying.

In each Nation contain set of generations or tribes, viz: *Otter*, *Bear*, *Wolf*, *Beaver*, *Turtle*. Each tribe has two chiefs to settle the disputes, etc. If a man commits murder, the nearest relation of the slain despatches the murderer with a war-club; the slain and the murderer are put in one grave. Sometimes their relation of the offender present a belt of white wampum, to make the atonement. The adulterous women are punished by shaving their heads, and banished from the town. The thieves are punished by whipping severely. To recover debts, they generally apply to the chiefs; the payments are made up by the relatives of the debtor. They have a certain time of worship; the false faces first commence the dances; they visit the houses to drive away sickness, etc. Each town or district are allowed to sacrifice a couple of white dogs: the dogs are painted and ornamented with strings of wampum; they throw the dogs into the fire and some tobacco, and addresses the Maker. They pretend to furnish him a coat of skin, and a pipe full of tobacco; after which have dances for several days. The private feats are guided by the dreams. The sixth family, Esaurora, or Tuscaroras, was visited by a person, and went to see their amusements, but he was abused by some of the ball-players. He punished the offender by throwing him into a tree; he suddenly disappeared, but the person came again and released the fellow from the tree. The visitor appeared very old man; he appeared among the people for a while; he taught them many things; how to respect their deceased friends, and to love their relations, etc., he informed the people that the whites beyond the great water had killed their Maker, but he rose again; and he warns them that the whites would in some future day take possession of the Big Island, and it was impossible to prevent it; the red children would melt away like snow before the heat. The aged became sick, and he told them to get different kinds of roots, to cure the diseases; and also showed them the manner of mourning, etc. The aged man died among them, and they buried him; but soon after some person went to the grave and found he had risen, and never heard of him since.

In the reign the King Atotarho IX, perhaps 350 years before the Columbus dis-covered the America. About this time the Kannea-stokaroneah or Erians A.D. 1150 sprung from the Senecas, and became numer-ous and powerful nation, occupying the country lying between the Genesee and Niagara Rivers. It was supposed that the national sovereignty was confirmed by the Senate of the Five Nations. A Queen, named Yagowanea, resided at the fort Kauhanauka, (said Tuscarora.) She had an influ-ence among the people, and extended her authority over twelve forts of the country. A treaty of peace was concluded between her and the Twakanhah, (Messissaugers.) After a time dissentions broke out between the Five Nations and the Messissaugers, and soon commenced hostilities: but the war was regulated under her control. The Queen lived out-side the fort in a long house, which was called a Peace House. She entertained the two parties who were at war with each other; indeed she was called the mother of the Nations. Each nation sent her a belt of wampum as a mark of respect, but where the Five Nations were engaged in the warfare she admitted two Canandaigua warriors into her house; and just as they began to smoke the pipe of peace a small party of the Messissaugers too came into the house. She betrayed her visitors—she advised the Messissaugers to kill the warriors, which was soon executed; the Messissaugers soon retired. The Queen was informed that two warriors of Canandaigua had been over the river and killed a young prince of the Messissaugers: this offense was too great to pass without condemning the murderers; the reason she gave them up. She immediately went and consulted the chieftain of the band, stationed at Kanhaitauneekay, east of Onondaga village, Buffalo reservation, and from thence repaired to fort Kauquatkay, situated on the lake Erie, the residence of the Kaunaquavouhar, a chief commander of the Erian forces. She dispatched two runners to assemble the people at Kauquatkay: the Queen too send an ambassy to form an alliance with the Naywaunaukauraunah, savage tribe, encamped on the lake Erie, to unite against the Five Nations. During the absence of the Queen from the fort Kauhanauka, a woman went privately and took a canoe and proceeded on

the lake Ontario, towards Canandaigua, as fast as
possible; she left the canoe at some place and went
through the woods, and came late in the evening
at Canandaigua, a fortified town, and immediately
informed the Governor, Shorihowane, that the
Erians were making preparations to destroy the
people living on the east side of Genesee river.
The woman gave directions how to send the spies:
the governor rose in the morning and sent out two
fast runners to the fort Kauhanauka, to ascertain
the matter; the two spies came to an old cornfield
south of the fort, where they met some boys hunting squirrels; the spies made inquiries and received
all necessary information respecting the Erian's
Council at Kauquatkay, and went home as fast
as possible. The Governor Sorihowane, obtained
the news. The business was so in haste that it was
impossible to procure any aid from the allies. He
collected the warriors from the neighboring forts,
amounting to fifteen hundred besides the women
and the old men. The governor separated the
people into three divisions; first the men, between
thirty and fifty years of age; second division, the
men were from twenty to thirty years of age; third
division, were women and old men. The Governor
had commanded the leaders to be in good courage
and use all the means in their power to defeat the

enemy. After parading the divisions they marched towards the Genesee River; the army halted at the fort Kawnesats, situated on a small lake east of Genesee. The governor had sent runners to observe the motions of the enemy. The women and old men were to remain at the fort to cook and provide provisions for the people. The runners came in and announced that the Erians had crossed the Genesee river; the divisions immediately proceeded and laid an ambush on both side the path; the first division was in front to commence the action at the advance of the enemy. With a stratagem a certain warrior was dressed with a bear skin, and was seated on the path a little distance from the front of the division, meanwhile the enemy came up and saw the bear sitting at ease; the enemy chase it, which brought them in the midst of the division; at once burst a most hideous yell, followed with a rattling of war clubs. After a severe contest the first division was compelled to retreat, but the assistance of the second company came up, and the battle was renewed. At last the Erians fled from the field, leaving six hundred warriors slain. The enemy hurried to cross the Genesee river; the Governor declined to chase the enemy, but returned to Canandaigua. About this time the King of the Five Nations had ordered the great war chief Shoribowane, (a Mohawk,) to

march directly with an army of five thousand warriors to aid the Governor of Canandaigua against
the Erians, to attack the fort Kauquatkay, endeavor
to extinguish the council fire of the enemy,
which was becoming dangerous to the neighboring nations; but unfortunately during the siege a
shower of arrows was flying from the fort, the
great war Chief Shorihowane was killed and his
body conveyed back to Genesee and was buried in
a solemn manner; but however, the siege continued
for several days. The Queen sued for peace—the
army immediately ceased from hostilities, and left
the Erians entire possession of the country. The
Skunantoh or Deer was the most useful game of
the Five Nations; the animal can run considerable
distance in a day. The people have a small dog in
aid to overtake, but very seldom stop when pursued by the dogs.

These creatures generally go in the river or
lake: in this situation the dogs are compelled to
leave the deer. The wolves are also prevented from
catching these animals: the hunters have never
seen a deer lying dead, except in some instances;
if a person find one it is considered a bad sign; his
wife had committed adultery, in consequence he
cannot kill any deer. When a person intends to hunt
deer he procures a medicine, and vomits once daily

for twelve days, after which he procures some pine or cedar boughs and boils them in a clay kettle, and after removed from the fire, he takes the blanket and covers himself over with it to sweat; the person that uses the medicine does not allow a woman with child or uncleanness to eat any of the venison. The people sometimes go out to hunt as the corn begins to grow on the ears; they make a long brush fence and remove the leaves on both sides of the fence, the deer will not follow the path; the person can easily kill the game. In the hot days of summer, they go and watch in the night at the salt licks. Another mode of killing the deer; they take slivers of basswood bark and proceed to the place and obtain a canoe and go into the river or lake in the night, provided with a light of slivers. The deer, elk and buffalo, were found in the territory of the Five Nations. The moose inhabit the spruce country and the heads of the Mohawk river; this country was never inhabited by any kind of people in the winter season; the snow fell so deep it was supposed that the country would always remain a wilderness.

About this time the Oneidas killed a very poisonous blue otter; the meat was very carefully preserved; some are used to hunt, and others to poison the arrows when go out to war; some of the witches obtained the meat to poison the people.

In the river and lakes are found various kinds of fishes. The people had particular time of the moon to make sugar, plant corn, and hunt deer and other animals. The seasons of the year they are directed by the seven stars of the heavens: when warriors travel in a great forest they are guided by a northern star; if the sun or moon is eclipsed they believe that the Bad Spirit darkens it: the people are assembled, and make a loud noise to scare the Bad Spirit from the orb. They believe that the clouds in the moon were earth and inhabited by people. The six family made resident near the mouth of Neuse river in North Carolina, and became three tribes, the Kautanohakau, Kauwetseka and Tuscarora, and united into a league and were at war with the Nanticokes, and totally on the sea shores. About this time the Long House became numerous and powerful; each nation could muster as follows: —the Mowhawks, 5,000 warriors; Oneidas, 3,500 warriors; Senecas, 6,000 warriors; Onondagas 4,000 warriors; Cayugas, 4,500 warriors; total amount 23,000 warriors. The Mowhawk was considered an oldest brother, and was appointed to keep a watch towards the sunrise, the Senecas were appointed to keep a watch towards the sunsetting. The Senators met annually, at the fort Onondaga, to promote their national prosperity.

The Long House were free and independent nations, and have been acknowledged in such treaties made with them by the neighboring nations. Every independent nation have a government of their own; they have a national committee meet occasionally; they have a chief ruler, named *Aukoyaner*, a peacemaker, who is invested with authority to administer the government. Each nation have a right to punish individuals of their own nation for offences, committed within their jurisdiction; each nation are bound to oppose any hostile invasions of the enemy.

In the reign Atotarho X, perhaps about 250 years before Columbus discovered America. The Oyalquarkeror, Big Bear, continue to

A.D.
1250

invade the country at Onondaga; a party went and encamped a day's journey distance from the village; they hunted and killed a few deer. One morning a woman left the camp and was going home to pound corn and to supply the men with provisions; but before she reached half way she was attacked by the monstrous Bear, and was soon devoured, as she did not return. The men were anxiously waiting, and were suspicious about

* *Aukoyaner*, i.e. Lord. No one can hold this office except a Turtle tribe, he governs the nation, but not allowed to go out to war, his duty is to stay home and preserve peace among his people.

60

her; a man was sent to see if she was coming; he advanced where she was assaulted, and discovered the place of her remains; he soon perceived their fate; he immediately reported and the men immediately proceeded to the place; and while examining her remains the bear made a vigorous attack; the men met a severe engagement, but in the meantime the monster was killed; they procured some of the meat for useful purposes.

Atotarho XI, perhaps about 150 years before Columbus discovered America. About this time the Tuscaroras sends messengers and renewed their intercourse *A.D. 1350* with the five nations. The Tuscaroras were yet numerous and had twenty-four large towns, and probably could muster six thousand warriors. They possessed the country lying between the sea shores and the mountains, which divide the Atlantic states; but afterwards a contest arose and the southern nations, the Oyatoh, Kwntariroraunuh, Caweda. The war lasted for many years; unfortunately it became so distressed that the Tuscaroras' frontier settlements were reduced considerably, but the Tuscaroras send expresses and received assistance from their brethren, the Five Nations, and war was carried on for some time; at last the enemy was compelled to suspend their hostility.

The Bear tribes nominate the Chief Warrior of the nation. The laws of the confederation provides the Onondagas to furnish a King and the Mowhawks a great war chief of the Five Nations.

About this time an earthquake was felt throughout the kingdom, supposed a large comet fell into some of the lakes; and other signs were seen in the heavens. The defender ceased from visiting the people in bodily form, but appeared to the prophet. In a dream he foretells the whites would cross the Big Waters and bring some liquors, and buy up the red people's lands; he advises them not to comply with the wishes of the whites, lest they should ruin themselves and displease their Maker; they would destroy the tree of peace and extinguish the Great Council Fire at Onondaga, which was so long preserved to promote their national sovereignty.

In the reign Atotarho XII, perhaps about 50 years before Columbus discovered America, the Tehatirihokea, or Mowhawks was at war with Ranatshaganha, supposed Mohegans, who occupied the opposite bank of the river Skaunataty or Hudson. The warfare was maintained by small expeditions; the Mowhawks would cross the river and attack the enemy; the canoes were kept in the river continually to cover their retreat; but after a while

A.D.
1450

the Mohegans expaliated the war: the chief of the Mowhawks received orders from the King, and invited the two confederate nations, the Oneidas and the Onondagas, to unite against the common enemy; the band of the combined forces immediately crossed the river and revenged a part of the country, and the enemy were compelled to sue for peace.

In the reign Atotarho XIII, in the year 1492, Columbus discovered the America. The Keatahkiehroneah were fighting with the neighboring tribes and were *A.D. 1500* injurious to the frontier settlements. The five nations sends Thoyenogea with an army of five thousand warriors and defeated the Keatahkiehroneah and drove them west of the Ohio River; and they lay waste the enemies' country, and attacked other tribes, etc. About this time the Erians declared a war against the Five Nations; a long bloody war ensued; at last the Erians were driven from the country, and supposed were incorporated with some of the southern nations; after which the kingdom enjoyed without disturbance for many years.

The Mowhawk was considered the oldest language of the confederacy.

Mowhawk.	Tuscarora.
1. Wus-kot.	1. Vntchee.
2. Tack-ny.	2. Nake-tee.
3. Au-suh.	3. Au-sh.
4. Kau-yaly	4. Hun-tock.
5. Wisk.	5. Whisk.
6. Yua-yak.	6. O-yak.
7. Gia-tock.	7. Gia-nock.
8. Sot-tai-gon.	8. Nake-ruh.
9. Tew-do.	9. Ni-ruh.
10. Oya-ly.	10. Wots-huh.

END.

The Massinahigan Series:
Brief Accounts of Early Native America

Volume 1
Brief History of King Philip's War 1675-1677,
by George M. Bodge (1891)

Volume 2
Sketches of Ancient History of the Six Nations,
by David Cusick (1825)

Volume 3
The Country of the Neutrals,
by James H. Coyne (1895)

Volume 4
*The Annual Narrative of the Mission of the Sault:
From Its Foundation Until the Year 1686*
by Claude Chauchetiere (1686)

Volume 5
*The Roman Rite in the Algonquian and Iroquoian
Missions From the Colonial Period to the Second
Vatican Council*
by Claudio R. Salvucci

For more information on this series, see our website at:
http://www.evolpub.com/Massinahigan/BAENA.html

www.ingramcontent.com/pod-product-compliance
Lightning Source LLC
Chambersburg PA
CBHW032106080426
42733CB00006B/448